Welcoming the Sabbath

Creative Projects, Rituals, and Recipes for Kids

Curriculum Materials Collection
Ratner Media Center
2030 South Taylor Road
Cleveland Heights, Ohio-44118

Written by Mark Falstein · Illustrate

RMC
241
FAL

12773

Falstein, Mark
Welcoming The Sabbath :
Creative Projects, Ritual
& Recipes for Kids

The Learning Works

Editing and Typography:
Kimberley A. Clark

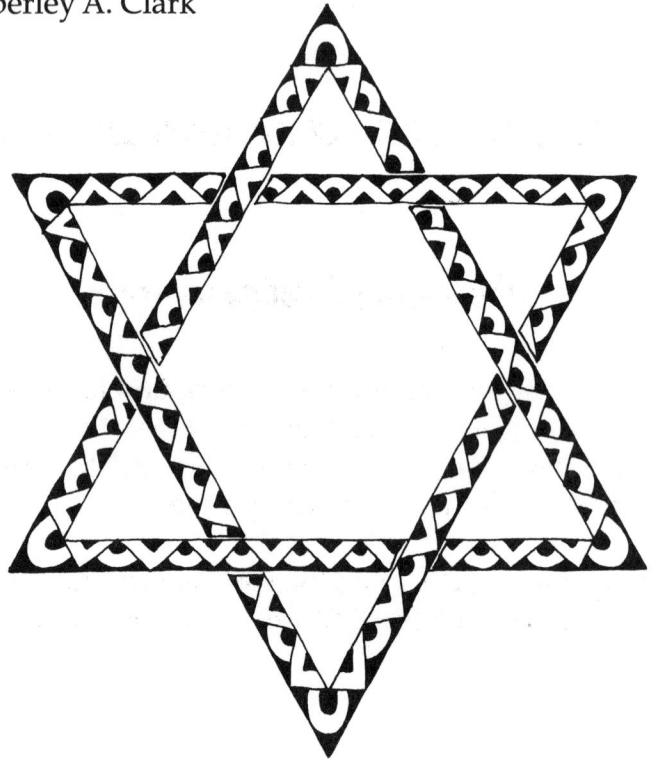

The purchase of this book entitles the individual teacher to reproduce copies for use in the classroom. The reproduction of any part for an entire school or school system or for commercial use is strictly prohibited. No form of this work may be reproduced, transmitted, or recorded without written permission from the publisher. Inquiries should be addressed to the Permissions Department.

Copyright © 1999
The Learning Works, Inc.
Santa Barbara, California 93160

ISBN: 0-88160-323-6
LW 386

Printed in the United States of America.

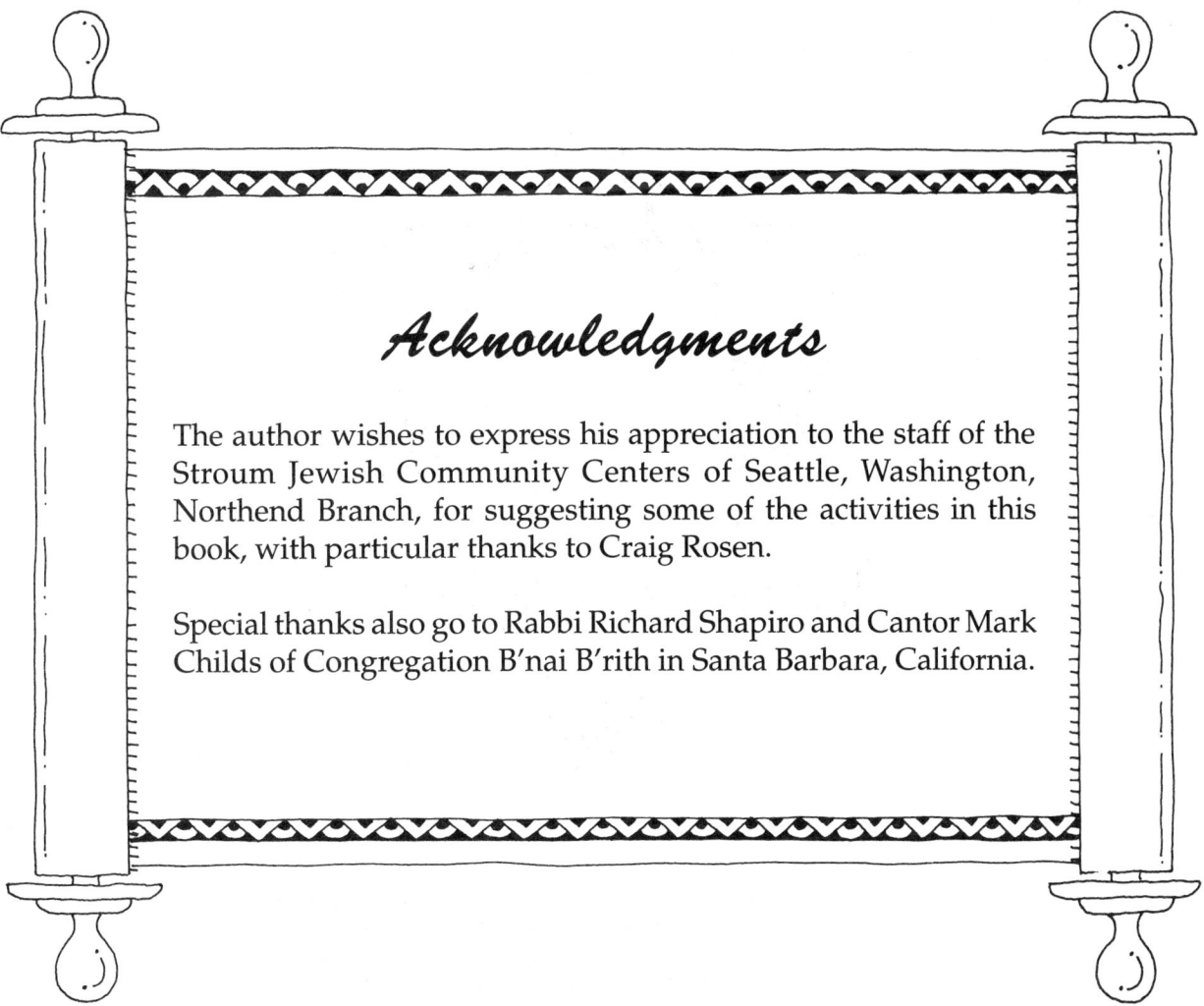

Acknowledgments

The author wishes to express his appreciation to the staff of the Stroum Jewish Community Centers of Seattle, Washington, Northend Branch, for suggesting some of the activities in this book, with particular thanks to Craig Rosen.

Special thanks also go to Rabbi Richard Shapiro and Cantor Mark Childs of Congregation B'nai B'rith in Santa Barbara, California.

Contents

Rituals

Preparing for Shabbat 8–9
Lighting Candles 10–11
Family Blessing 12
Kiddush 13
Motzi 14–15
The Festive Meal 16–17
The Cycle of Work and Rest 18–19
Prayer and Study 20–21
Shabbat Meditation 22–23
Performing Mitzvot 24–25
Havdalah 26

Family Projects

"I Remember Shabbat" 28–29
Organize a Shabbat Picnic 30
Z'mirot 31
Ask Me Another 32
Fill Me In 33
Take a Creation Walk 34–35
Go-Filte-Fish: A Card Game 36–41
Family Tikkun Olam Project 42
Jewish Community Worldwide 43
Family Shabbat Journal 44

Welcoming the Sabbath
© The Learning Works, Inc.

Contents

Arts and Crafts

Make a Challah Cover	46
Hebrew Name Place Cards	47
Twelve Tribes Cups	48–49
Make a Shabbat Mural	50
Jewish Jigsaw Puzzle	51
Scenes From the Parashiot	52–53
Stained-Glass Windows	54
A Thousand Words Are Worth a Picture	55
Mezuzah Growth Chart	56
Hebrew Alphabet Patterns	57
Make Havdalah Candles	58

Recipes

Challah for Shabbat	60–61
A Little Chicken Soup	62–63
Liverless Chopped Liver	64
Tabbuleh	65
Roast Chicken and Vegetables	66–67
Bubbe's Mandelbroit	68–69
Favorite Fruit Salads	70
Hummos	71
Baklava	72

Introduction

Shabbat Shalom! ***Welcoming the Sabbath*** is a book of projects, family fun, and Jewish thoughts to add to your enjoyment of that special day at the end of the week. Some of the activities are meant to be done alone, while others can be done with your family or with friends and neighbors. Each activity will remind you that Shabbat is a day set aside, a day of "time out" from the rest of the week.

Not all of these activities are meant to be done *on* Shabbat. (Observant Jews will notice that some of them cannot be done on Shabbat under Jewish law.) Some of them are meant to help you prepare *for* Shabbat. Others will keep you thinking *about* Shabbat. And there are still others that can be enjoyed at any time, but which will add a special flavor to that special day.

There are four kinds of activities in this book.

> **Rituals:** Blessings, prayers, interesting facts, and ideas for thought and discussion to help you connect with the 3,500-year tradition of Shabbat.
>
> **Family projects:** Games, outings, and other activities to help make Shabbat a special day for your whole family.
>
> **Arts and crafts:** Easy-to-do projects for decorating your home and Shabbat dinner table.
>
> **Recipes:** Step-by-step instructions for preparing treats for your Shabbat meals.

You can begin by sharing some of the activities with your family. Choose where you'd like to begin. It's Friday afternoon. The sun is about to set. It's time to slow down—time to get into that special mood. It's time for Shabbat!

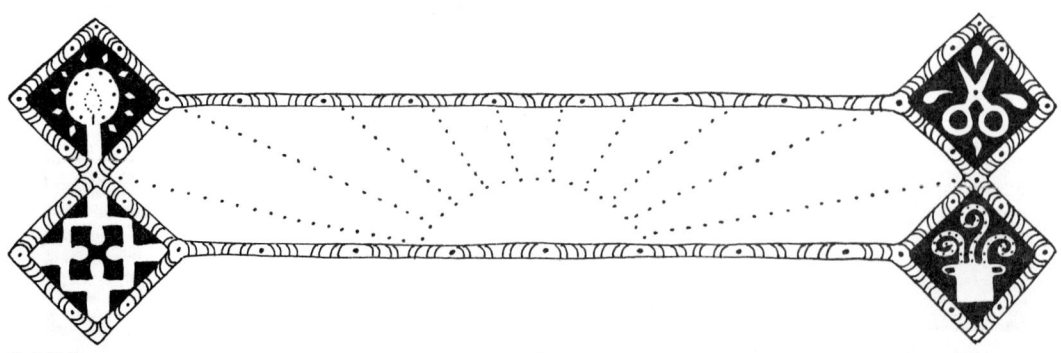

Preparing for Shabbat

The word *shabbat* in Hebrew means "to stop" or "to pause." It is the day when Jews take time out from the business and *busy*-ness of the week to get in touch with the important things in life. It is a day to focus on our loved ones and on our feelings about the universe and its Creator.

The traditional Hebrew greeting for Shabbat is *Shabbat Shalom*. "Shalom" has many meanings, one of which is "completeness." How can you bring about a feeling of completeness on Shabbat? Here are a few ideas:

- Plan to have all your day's activities finished an hour or more before Shabbat begins. Take some time to think about what Shabbat means to you and to get into that special Shabbat feeling.

- Dress in your best clothes. (White is a traditional Shabbat color.)

- Help your family prepare for a special dinner. Lay a clean tablecloth, polish the candlesticks, decorate the table with flowers. Do some extra chores to help your family get ready to separate from the cares of the week.

Preparing for Shabbat

Think and Talk

What else can you do to prepare for Shabbat? Here are a few ideas to talk about with your family.

- The Fourth Commandment reminds Jews to "keep Shabbat holy." What does *holy* mean to you?

- Jews traditionally have called Shabbat "the bride" or "the queen." What does this tell us about how we can welcome Shabbat?

- In your Bible, read Genesis 2:1-3 and Exodus 31:16-17. What ideas do these passages give us for observing Shabbat?

What other ways can you and your family think of to prepare for Shabbat?

Lighting Candles

Jews usher in Shabbat by lighting candles at home. This ceremony reminds us that the home is central to Jewish life. It also creates a link with Jews throughout the world and reminds us that Shabbat is a day apart from the concerns of the week.

The mitzvah of lighting candles is traditionally performed by women. The ancient law codes, however, oblige both men and women to light candles. In many households, all members of the family light candles together.

The candle-lighter traditionally "gathers in the light" by bringing it toward her three times with her hands before reciting the blessing.

By custom, the candle-lighter covers her eyes while saying the blessing. Shabbat begins when the blessing is complete and the candles are "revealed" as lit.

Welcoming the Sabbath
© The Learning Works, Inc.

Lighting Candles

Baruch atta, Adonai   בָּרוּךְ אַתָּה, יְיָ

eloheinu, melekh ha-olam,   אֱלֹהֵינוּ, מֶלֶךְ הָעוֹלָם,

asher kid'shanu b'mitzvotav   אֲשֶׁר קִדְּשָׁנוּ בְּמִצְוֹתָיו,

v'tsivanu l'hadlik ner shel Shabbat.   וְצִוָּנוּ לְהַדְלִיק נֵר שֶׁל שַׁבָּת.

You are blessed, Eternal our G-d, ruler of the universe,
who has made us holy by your commandments,
and commanded us to kindle the lights of Shabbat

Think and Talk

- Most families use at least two candles. They symbolize the two commands to "remember" (*zakhor*) and to "keep" (*shamor*) Shabbat, from the two different versions of the Ten Commandments (Exodus 20 and Deuteronomy 5). Some families add more candles, one for each family member or guest.

- Orthodox Jewish law allows us to bring in Shabbat up to one and a quarter hours before sunset. Once the candles are lit, it is Shabbat, whether or not the sun has set.

- Traditionally, most *mitzvot* in Jewish ritual have been performed by men. Why do women usually light the Shabbat candles?

Welcoming the Sabbath
© The Learning Works, Inc.

Family Blessing

In many families, parents bless their children as Shabbat begins. The blessing for boys is taken from Jacob's blessing of his grandsons, Ephraim and Menasheh. The blessing for girls recalls the four mothers of Israel: Sarah, Rebekah, Rachel, and Leah.

Ephraim and Menasheh are held as examples because they are the first brothers mentioned in the Bible who did not fight with each other.

The Bible presents women whose decisions and actions helped to shape and guide their people. This is unusual among ancient writings.

for boys:

Y'sim'kha Elohim k'Ephraim

v'khiMenasheh.

יְשִׂמְךָ אֱלוֹהִים כְּאֶפְרַיִם

וְכִמְנַשֶּׁה.

for girls:

Y'simekh Elohim k'Sarah,

Rivkah, Rachel, v'Leah.

יְשִׂמֵךְ אֱלוֹהִים כְּשָׂרָה,

רִבְקָה, רָחֵל, וְלֵאָה.

May G-d make you like Ephraim and Menasheh.
May G-d make you like Sarah, Rebekah, Rachel, and Leah.

Think and Talk

- What is a blessing? In what ways do you feel blessed? In what ways would you wish to bless others?

- How might you change the traditional family blessing to make it more meaningful for your family and to include blessings for all?

Welcoming the Sabbath
© The Learning Works, Inc.

Kiddush

Kiddush means *sanctification*—setting something apart as holy. Wine is traditionally used for kiddush, but kiddush is not a sanctification of wine. It *uses* wine to sanctify Shabbat.

The blessing which we call kiddush was written by rabbis nearly 2,000 years ago, to fulfill the commandment to "keep Shabbat holy."

In Jewish tradition, wine is a symbol of joy. It is used in the kiddush to declare the specialness of the day. Grape juice may be used instead.

The kiddush for Shabbat is in three parts: a paragraph from the Book of Genesis describing the first Sabbath; the one-sentence blessing over wine (shown below); and the longer blessing sanctifying the day of Shabbat.

Baruch atta, Adonai	בָּרוּךְ אַתָּה, יְיָ
eloheinu, melekh ha-olam,	אֱלוֹהֵנוּ, מֶלֶךְ הָעוֹלָם,
borei p'ri ha-gafen.	בּוֹרֵא פְּרִי הַגָּפֶן.

You are blessed, Eternal our G-d, ruler of the universe,
who creates the fruit of the vine.

Think and Talk

- Use a special cup for kiddush. Read the full text of the kiddush from a *siddur* (prayer book) in Hebrew or English. Let everyone have a taste of the kiddush wine or grape juice. What else could serve as a symbol for joy?

- The kiddush calls Shabbat a gift of G-d, a reminder of the act of creation, and a reminder of the exodus from Egypt. How is Shabbat each of these things?

Welcoming the Sabbath
© The Learning Works, Inc.

Motzi

Jews traditionally say the blessing over bread, or *motzi*, at every meal. The blessing is special on Shabbat only because the day is special. The blessing is an expression of thanks for G-d's plenty, an expression of faith that "G-d will provide," and a reminder of the act of creation.

In traditional Judaism, it is a custom for everyone to wash their hands at the table before motzi is said, or to symbolize this act by dipping their fingers in water. Many families today do not use this custom, believing it is no longer relevant.

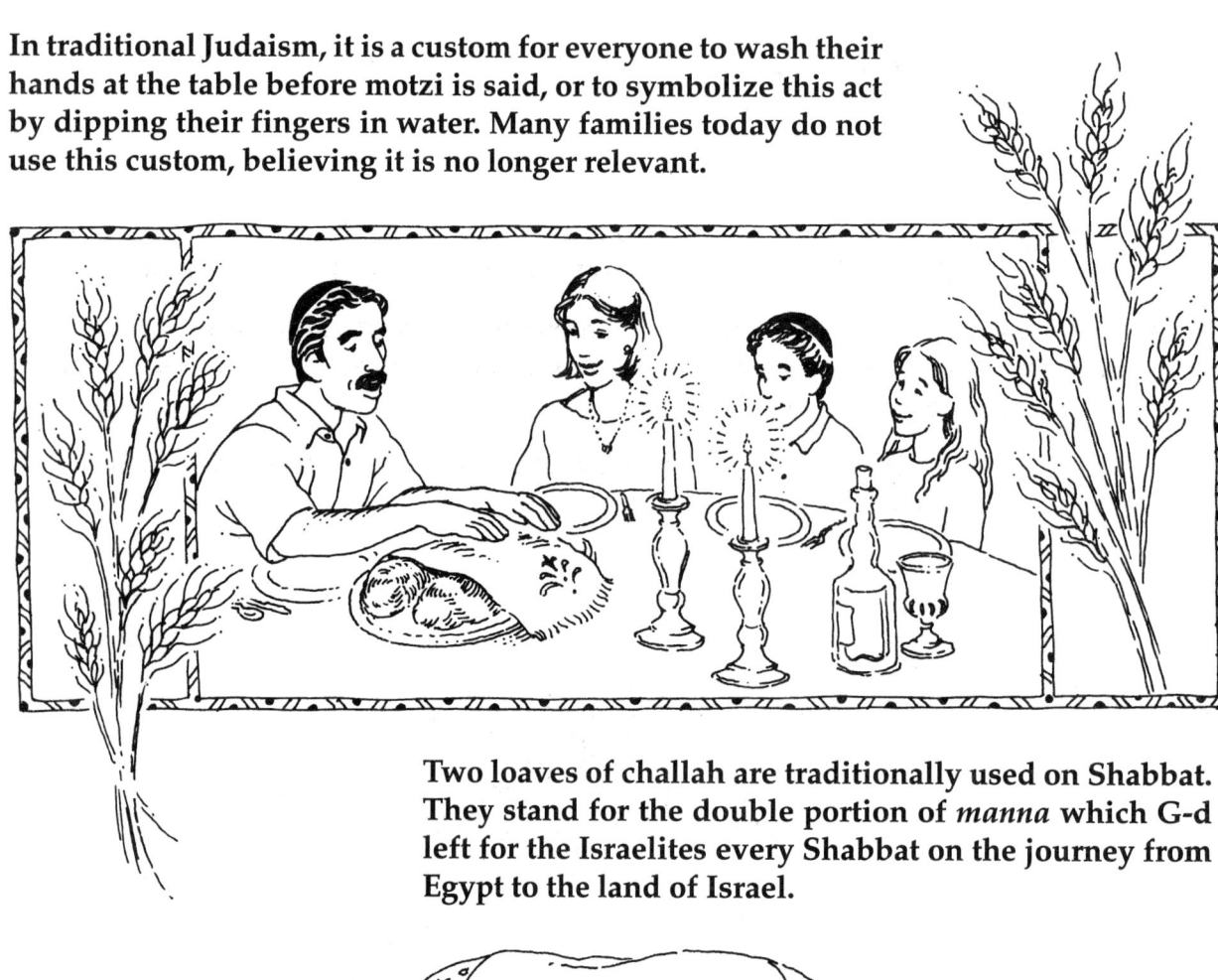

Two loaves of challah are traditionally used on Shabbat. They stand for the double portion of *manna* which G-d left for the Israelites every Shabbat on the journey from Egypt to the land of Israel.

Welcoming the Sabbath
© The Learning Works, Inc.

Motzi

Baruch atta, Adonai

eloheinu, melekh ha-olam,

hamotzi lechem min ha-aretz.

בָּרוּךְ אַתָּה, יְיָ

אֱלֹהֵינוּ, מֶלֶךְ הָעוֹלָם,

הַמּוֹצִיא לֶחֶם מִן הָאָרֶץ.

You are blessed, Eternal our G-d, ruler of the universe,
who brings bread out of the earth.

Think and Talk

- G-d does not actually "bring bread out of the earth." God lets wheat grow, and we turn it into bread. In what other ways do we share in the act of creation?

- In saying the *motzi*, we give thanks for food brought forth from the bare ground. In earlier times, people thought of this as a miracle. What other "miracles" do we have to be thankful for?

- The Hebrew word for bread, *lechem*, has the same root as the word *milchamah*, "war." What does this suggest to you?

The Festive Meal

A special meal on Shabbat is more than a good idea—it's the Law! Deuteronomy 8:10 instructs Jews to "eat, be satisfied and bless the Eternal." The Talmud uses the term *se'udat mitzvah* to describe the Shabbat meal—a festive dinner which involves fulfilling certain commandments. Help your family make preparing and eating Shabbat dinner a truly special occasion.

Rabbi Shammai, in the first century B.C.E., began the tradition of feasting on Shabbat. He would start early in the week to search for the finest ingredients.

The Shabbat meal does not have to be fancy to be special. Simple dinners can be delicious, especially when accompanied by blessings.

The Festive Meal

It is a tradition to conclude a meal with the *birkat ha-mazon*—the blessing after the meal. If this is not your custom, try this shorter version:

Baruch atta, Adonai,   בָּרוּךְ אַתָּה, יְיָ,

hazan et-hakol   הַזָּן אֶת הַכֹּל.

You are blessed, Eternal One, who feeds all.

Think and Talk

- What subjects would and would not be appropriate to talk about at the Shabbat table?

- You and and your family lead busy lives. How could you make it easier to make time for a festive Shabbat dinner in your weekly routine?

- It has always been considered a mitzvah to invite a stranger into your home for Shabbat dinner. How could your family do this?

- In a siddur, read the complete *birkat ha-mazon* with your family in Hebrew or English. Why does it combine thanks for food with thanks for the land of Israel, Jerusalem, and a prayer for peace?

The Cycle of Work and Rest

Shabbat is traditionally called the "day of rest." It is a day when Jews leave off "all kinds of work." But what is rest? What is work? While the Talmud lists many activities which are forbidden as work on Shabbat, it doesn't provide much direction after that. Non-observant Jews follow their own guidelines about work, but they often find it hard to know how to rest! How can you and your family truly make Shabbat a day of rest?

Many Jewish families take a leisurely walk around the neighborhood after synagogue services on Saturday.

Studying alone or with a group on Shabbat afternoon is considered a mitzvah—and so is taking a nap!

Spending quiet time with family or friends is a traditional way to rest on Shabbat.

Welcoming the Sabbath
© The Learning Works, Inc.

The Cycle of Work and Rest

Think and Talk

- "G-d rested on the seventh day." Talk about what G-d's resting might suggest to us about our own Shabbat activities.

- Sit down with your family and make a list of "dos" and "don'ts" that can help make Shabbat special for you. What restful activities can you do that you never seem to have time for during the week? What activities might you *not* do in order to make Shabbat seem more special?

- Ask family members what sort of "family rest activities" they would enjoy. Tell them what kinds of activities you would like. Over several Shabbats, make a point of honoring or sharing in each other's chosen activities.

Prayer and Study

According to the Talmud, Torah study is equal to all other *mitzvot* combined, "because it leads to them all." Jews study Torah in synagogue, but the home is a place of study, too—and when better than on Shabbat? Make some form of Torah study a part of your Shabbat every week.

One traditional Jewish view of heaven is a place where people can study Torah without being bothered with worldly things.

The synagogue has three traditional names: *bet midrash*, "house of study," *bet t'filah*, "house of prayer," and *bet k'nesset*, "house of meeting."

"What is hateful to you, do not do to other people. That is the whole of Torah. All the rest is commentary. Go and study it."

—Hillel

Welcoming the Sabbath
© The Learning Works, Inc.

Prayer and Study

Think and Talk

- Go to synagogue services with your family. Talk about the various prayers and parts of the service and what they mean to you. Attend services at a different synagogue than your own. What are some of the things that are done differently? What things are the same?

- At home, read the *parasha* (Torah portion) for the week. Let everyone in the family talk about the parasha. What are some of the lessons it contains for people today? Read the *haftarah* that accompanies the week's parasha. Can you think of why the rabbis might have chosen to group the two readings together?

- Get together with one or two other families for a session of Torah study. How can studying with others help you better understand what you are reading?

- Learn five new Hebrew words every Shabbat.

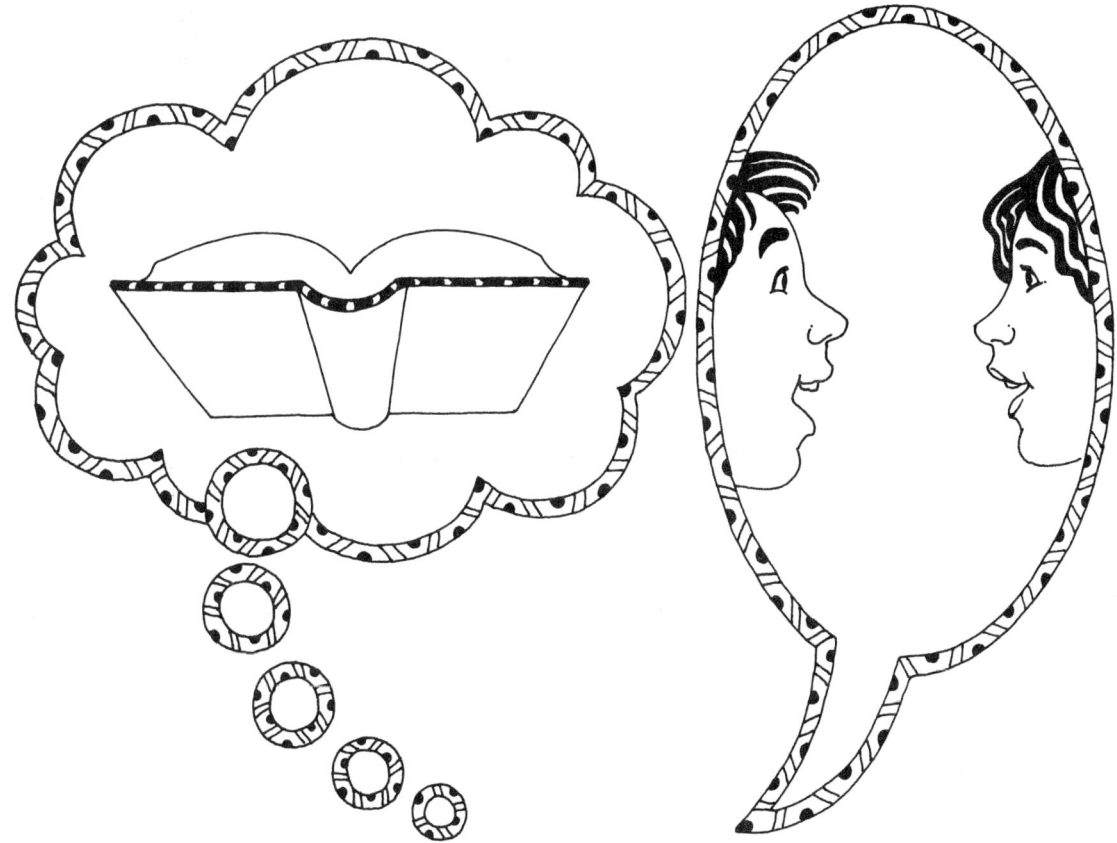

Shabbat Meditation

Jews usually pray, study, and celebrate holidays as members of a community. Traditionally, there can be no official prayer service without 10 Jews of *bar mitzvah* age. (Most Jews today also include girls of bat mitzvah age in their counting.) But that doesn't mean you can't pray during your quiet times alone. Those can be the best times to think about how you feel about G-d, the universe, everything outside yourself.

"When I consider your heavens, the work of your fingers ... what is a human being, that you should care about him? ... Yet you have made him a little lower than the angels."

—*Psalm 8*

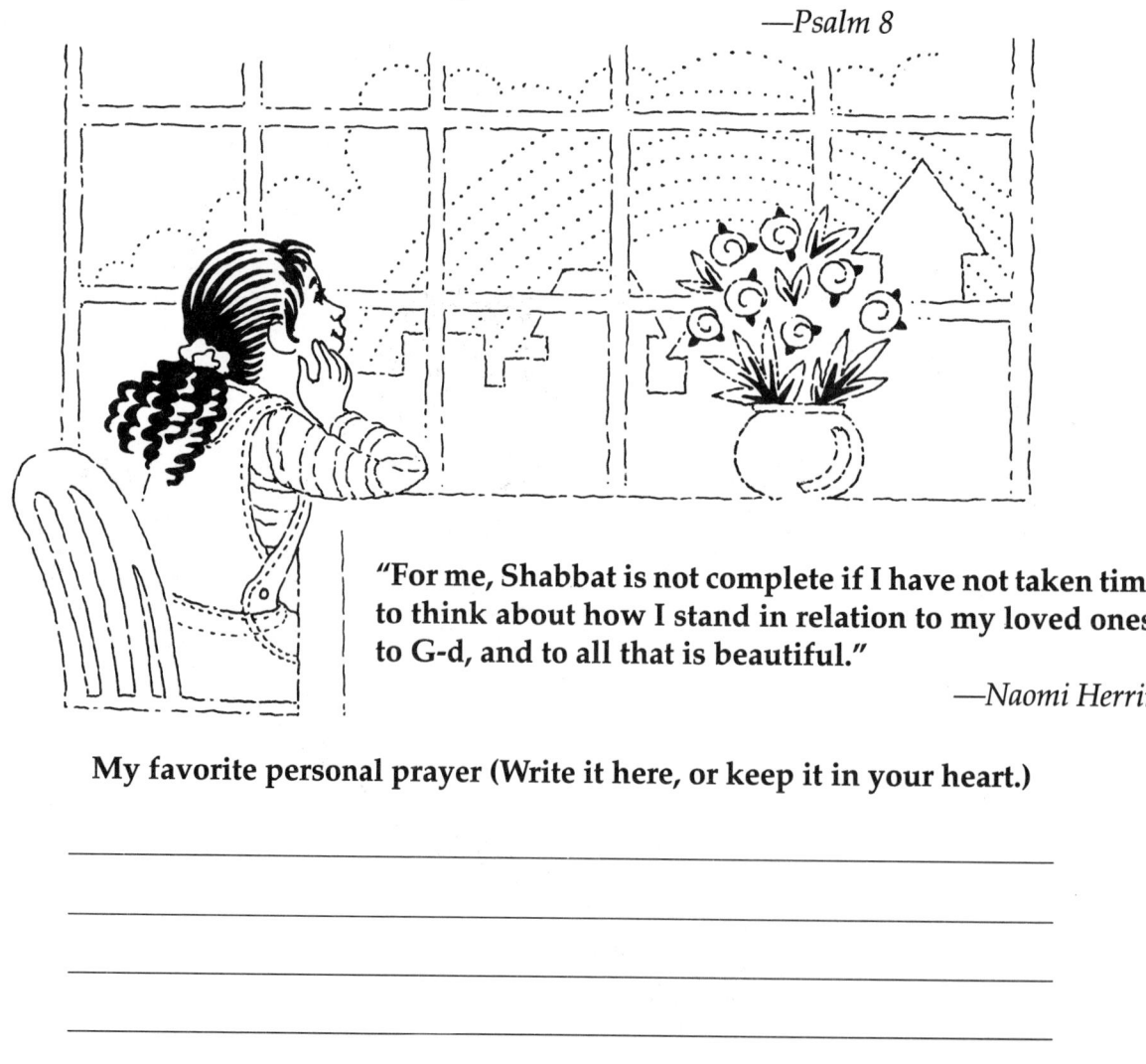

"For me, Shabbat is not complete if I have not taken time to think about how I stand in relation to my loved ones, to G-d, and to all that is beautiful."

—*Naomi Herrin*

My favorite personal prayer (Write it here, or keep it in your heart.)

_____
_____
_____
_____
_____

Shabbat Meditation

Things to Think About

- People pray to ask G-d for something, and they pray to thank G-d for something. What other kinds of prayer can you think of?

- Think about your own personal "thoughts of the spirit." You might want to keep a small notebook or journal to write them down. Think about your own personal beliefs about G-d, about your family, about your place in the universe. Think about special memories that you treasure.

Performing Mitzvot

The Hebrew word *mitzvah* means "commandment." Yet a mitzvah is something we choose, not something that we are ordered to do. A mitzvah is something that comes from the heart in response to G-d and Jewish tradition. For example, choosing to make Shabbat special is a mitzvah. Sharing Shabbat joy with others is a mitzvah. An act of kindness is a mitzvah. Choosing to "do the right thing" when the wrong thing may be easier is a mitzvah.

"If I am not for myself, who will be for me? But if I am only for myself, what am I? And if not now, when?"
—Hillel

Visiting the sick is a traditional mitzvah on Shabbat. The Talmud lists it as one of ten special acts for which a person is rewarded "in this world and the world to come."

Performing Mitzvot

Think and Talk

- A mitzvah may be either something you do or something you don't do. Think of a few examples of each.

- A mitzvah may be something you do for yourself or something you do for others. Think of a few examples of each.

- Jewish tradition says that doing one mitzvah will lead to another and another. Why do you suppose this is so?

- Some of the acts we think of as mitzvot might be considered "work" according to traditional Jewish law. Make two lists. Make one of them "Mitzvot for Shabbat." Make the other "Mitzvot for Weekdays."

Havdalah

Havdalah means "separation." It is the name of the ceremony that ends Shabbat. In making havdalah, Jews remember that G-d separates the holy from the ordinary and Shabbat from the rest of the week. To perform the havdalah ceremony, you need wine or juice, a box containing fragrant spices, and a special braided candle.

Smelling the spices is a reminder that, although Shabbat is ending, it will come again. If you don't have a spice box, you can use an orange pierced with cloves.

The havdalah candle has many wicks joined together. It stands for the separation of light and darkness, understanding and confusion.

According to the Talmud, Shabbat is over when it is dark enough to see three stars. (Planets don't count.) Part of the havdalah ceremony includes these words:

Baruch atta, Adonai,   בָּרוּךְ אַתָּה, יְיָ,

ha-mavdil bein kodesh l'chol.   הַמַּבְדִּיל בֵּין קֹדֶשׁ לְחוֹל.

You are blessed, Eternal One,
who separates the holy from the ordinary.

Think and Talk

- Read the havdalah ceremony in a siddur. Enjoy havdalah with your family at the end of Shabbat.

- Havdalah separates Shabbat from the rest of the week. What other "separations between the holy and the ordinary" can you think of?

- Havdalah is a good time to think about how you will live the next week in the spirit of Shabbat.

"I Remember Shabbat"

Jews everywhere celebrate Shabbat, but not all Jews do it in the same way. Here is an oral-history project that can involve the whole family in learning how Jews in your community and elsewhere observe the holy day. You'll need:

- pen and paper
- cassette tape recorder and a blank tape
- *optional:* camera, video camera

1. You will be asking people questions about how their families observed Shabbat when they were young. Some of the questions you'll want to ask include:

    - How was Shabbat observed in your home and community?

    - Where and when was this?

    - What foods did your family traditionally eat at Shabbat dinner?

    - What Shabbat experiences do you best remember?

    Think of more questions you'll want to ask your subjects. Jot them down here.

"I Remember Shabbat"

2. Start by asking your parents, grandparents, and other relatives and neighbors about their Shabbat memories. Ask if they remember stories their own parents or grandparents told them about Shabbat. Record their responses. Be sure to include the date of each interview and the subject's name. Get permission from the people you interview before photographing or tape-recording them.

3. Use resources in your synagogue or Jewish Community Center to contact other members of the Jewish community, especially those who were born in other countries. If possible, have your parents arrange to take you to a Jewish senior center or other place where older people gather.

4. Have the whole family participate in editing your interviews. Organize them in book form or as a taped or mixed-media archive.

Organize a Shabbat Picnic

Share your Shabbat dinner with several families. For those warm summer Friday evenings when you want to be outdoors, why not make it a picnic? Organizing a meal with several families will take planning. Read the steps below to help you get started.

1. Talk with neighbors or family friends about the idea. Decide on a date and a location. For a picnic, you may need to reserve a site. Call your local parks and recreation department to find out what's required.

2. Have a short planning meeting a week or so before the event. At least one member of each participating family should attend. (You could also make arrangements over the phone.) Among the items you'll want to discuss are:

    - What will you eat and drink, and who will bring each item? What else will you need?

    - Who will provide candle holders, candlesticks, and a kiddush cup? Do you want to choose someone to lead the *brakhot*, or will you take turns?

    - What sort of entertainment will you provide? It can be special to Shabbat or simply for fun. Does anyone have a Hebrew song book? Can anyone lead the songs or play an instrument? What games can you play?

    - Will you include Torah study or a discussion of some topic? Find out who would be willing to guide such a discussion.

    - Have an alternate plan in case it rains.

3. Help your family prepare for the event. Call the other families a day or two before and discuss any changes that may have to be made. Have fun!

Observant Jews may wish to talk to a rabbi to consider how this activity might be changed to conform to *halakhah*.

Welcoming the Sabbath
© The Learning Works, Inc.

Z'mirot

Zemer is the Hebrew word for "music," and *z'mirot* are simple songs sung around the Shabbat table after dinner. You may feel self-conscious at first about singing *z'mirot*, but give it a try. You don't know any? Start with this list of titles. You may remember having learned some of these songs at one time. Your parents may also be familiar with some of them.

"David Melekh Yisrael"
(David, king of Israel, lives and will rise again)

"Hineh ma tov"
(Behold, how good and how pleasant it is for brothers to live together in unity)

"Am Yisrael Chai"
(The Jewish people live)

"Bim Bam/Shabbat Shalom"

A Jewish bookstore or mail-order house will have books containing these songs and many others.

Here are some other activities to try:

- Get a few recordings of traditional or modern songs suitable for Shabbat. Make a tape of your favorites and sing along.

- Learn a new Shabbat song in Hebrew or English and teach it to your family.

- Write lyrics and music for your own Shabbat song, or write words to a familiar tune.

- Learn an Israeli or traditional Hasidic dance and teach it to your family.

Ask Me Another

Do you know that many chess champions have been Russian Jews? Some people say that it's because a rabbi made a ruling 200 years ago that permitted chess-playing on Shabbat. If chess is okay, how much more so are games that showcase your Jewish learning? Here are two to play with your family and friends, based on the classic games "20 Questions" and "Categories."

What You Do

1. One player thinks of an item from Jewish life. The only clue he or she gives the others is whether the item is animal (such as Samson's hair), vegetable (such as the Passover afikomen) or mineral (such as the Western Wall).

2. The other player or players must guess the item in 20 questions or less. Only "yes or no" questions are allowed.

3. If no one guesses correctly, the first player gets another turn.

Fill Me In

What You Do

1. In this game, players fill categories with names or words beginning with specific letters. Each player starts by marking off a grid with five horizontal and vertical columns.

2. Players take turns naming categories to use. Each category must have some connection to Jewish life. Write the categories at the heads of the vertical columns.

3. Draw five letters from a bag. (Use letter tiles from store-bought games, or letters written on scraps of paper.) Write them in front of the horizontal rows.

	ritual objects	places in Israel	Jewish sports stars	books of the Bible	song titles
A	afikomen	Ashkelon	Amy Alcott	Amos	Am Yisrael Chai
K	kiddush cup		Sandy Koufax	Kings	
G		Galilee		Genesis	

4. Decide on a time limit for filling in the grid. Use a kitchen timer or watch. A player scores 1 point for each square he or she fills correctly, and earns a 5-point bonus for filling in all the letter squares in one category. The player with the highest score wins.

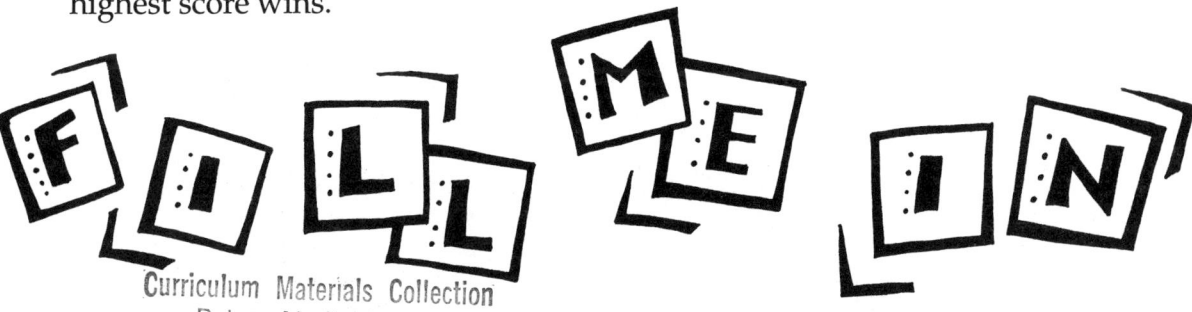

Take a Creation Walk

Take an early-morning walk! A walk on Shabbat is traditional, and this one will let you celebrate, literally, all creation.

1. Prepare for the walk by reading the first chapter of Genesis with your family.
2. Talk about what you can do on a morning walk to observe and appreciate what G-d created on each day of creation. Limit your plan to what you can do in your neighborhood, or wherever you will be spending Shabbat. Jot down your ideas below. Use a separate sheet of paper if you need more space.

Day	What G-d created	How we can celebrate
1	light; day and night	Get out of the house before dawn to greet the light
2	the sky	
3	the sea and dry land; plants	
4	the sun, moon, planets, and stars	
5	creatures of the sky and sea	
6	land animals (including people)	
7	Shabbat	

Welcoming the Sabbath
© The Learning Works, Inc.

Take a Creation Walk

3. Refer to your list of ideas as you plan the route for your walk. Choose the best spot in your neighborhood to celebrate each day. The "days" need not come in any particular order. For example, you may stop and identify constellations and stars (day 4) before you appreciate the beauty of the dawn sky (day 2).

Go-Filte-Fish: A Card Game

For many Jews, *gefilte* (stuffed) fish is a favorite dish on Shabbat and holidays. Go-Filte-Fish also is a card game, based on the classic game of "go fish." It's fun to play on Shabbat afternoon or anytime.

Setting Up the Game

1. Reproduce the Go-Filte-Fish cards on pages 37–41. Glue each section of cards to a sheet of cardboard.

2. Carefully cut out the individual cards. You'll have 52 of them, just like a standard deck of cards, but instead of aces, face cards, and numbered cards, you'll have four-card sets, each illustrated with one of the following: a menorah, a torah scroll, candlesticks, challah, a talit, a Star of David, a shofar, tablets of the law, the Western Wall, a kiddush cup, a spice box, a map of Israel, and a mezuzah.

Welcoming the Sabbath
© The Learning Works, Inc.

Go-Filte-Fish: A Card Game

How to Play

1. Two to six people can play. If there are two to four players, deal seven cards to each player; if there are more than four players, deal four cards to each player. The rest of the cards are spread out in the middle of the table to form the fish pond.

2. Play proceeds in turns, beginning at the dealer's left. The player whose turn it is asks any other player if she has any of a particular card, for example: "Shira, do you have any shofars?" The asker may only ask for cards that he or she has. Here, for example, he must have at least one shofar card.

3. If the player asked has any of the cards asked for, she must give them to the asker. If she does not, she says "Go-Filte-Fish," and the asker must draw a card from the fish pond.

4. If the asker is successful in getting the card he asks for, either from another player or from the fish pond, he gets another turn. (*Variation:* the player gets an extra turn only when he completes a set of four cards.)

5. A player completing a set of four cards shows them to the other players and places them face down in a pile. Play continues until all the cards are formed into sets. The player with the most sets wins.

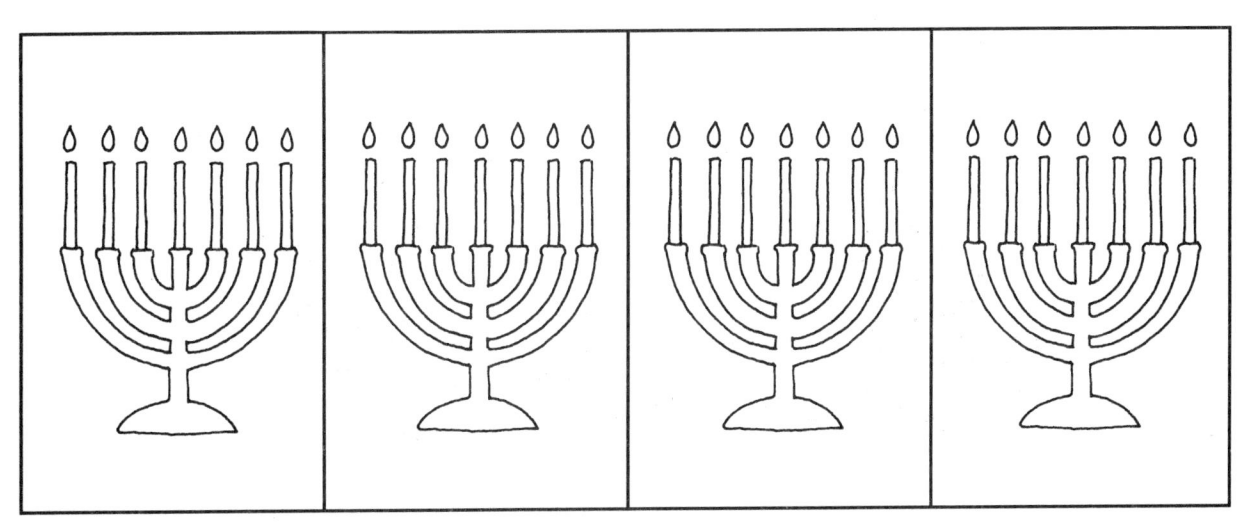

Go-Filte-Fish Cards

Go-Filte-Fish Cards

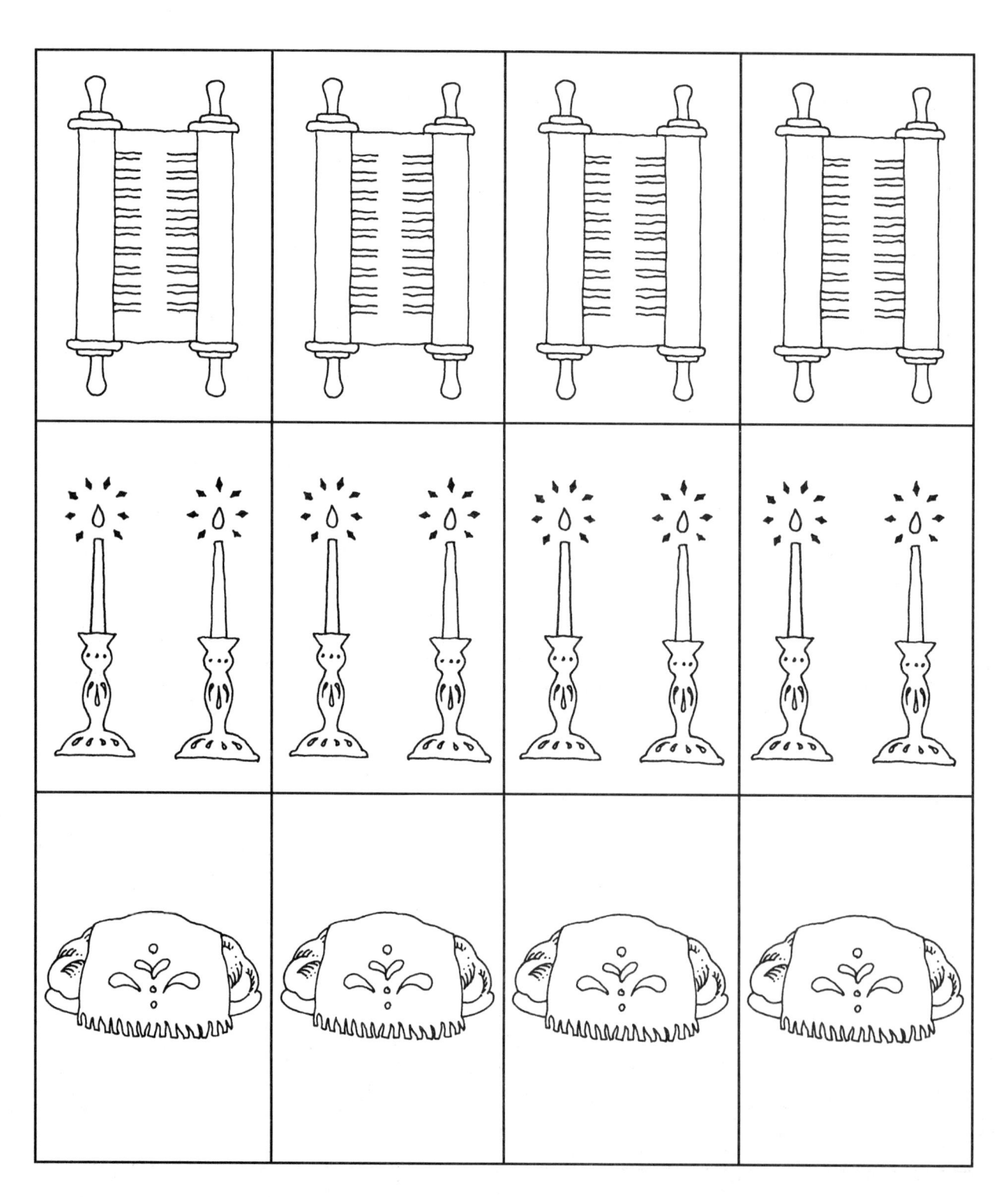

Welcoming the Sabbath
© The Learning Works, Inc.

Go-Filte-Fish Cards

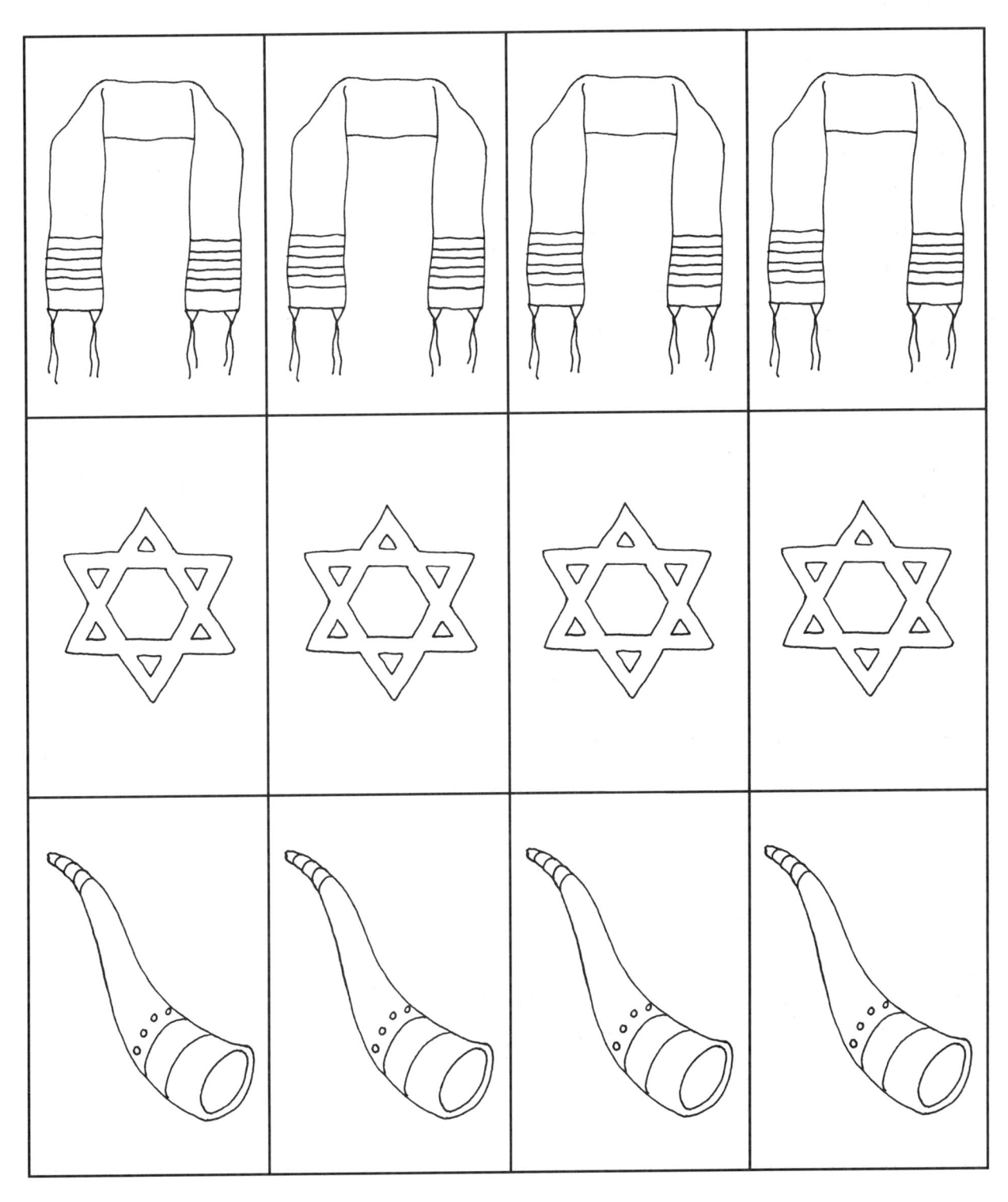

Go-Filte-Fish Cards

Welcoming the Sabbath
© The Learning Works, Inc.

Go-Filte-Fish Cards

41

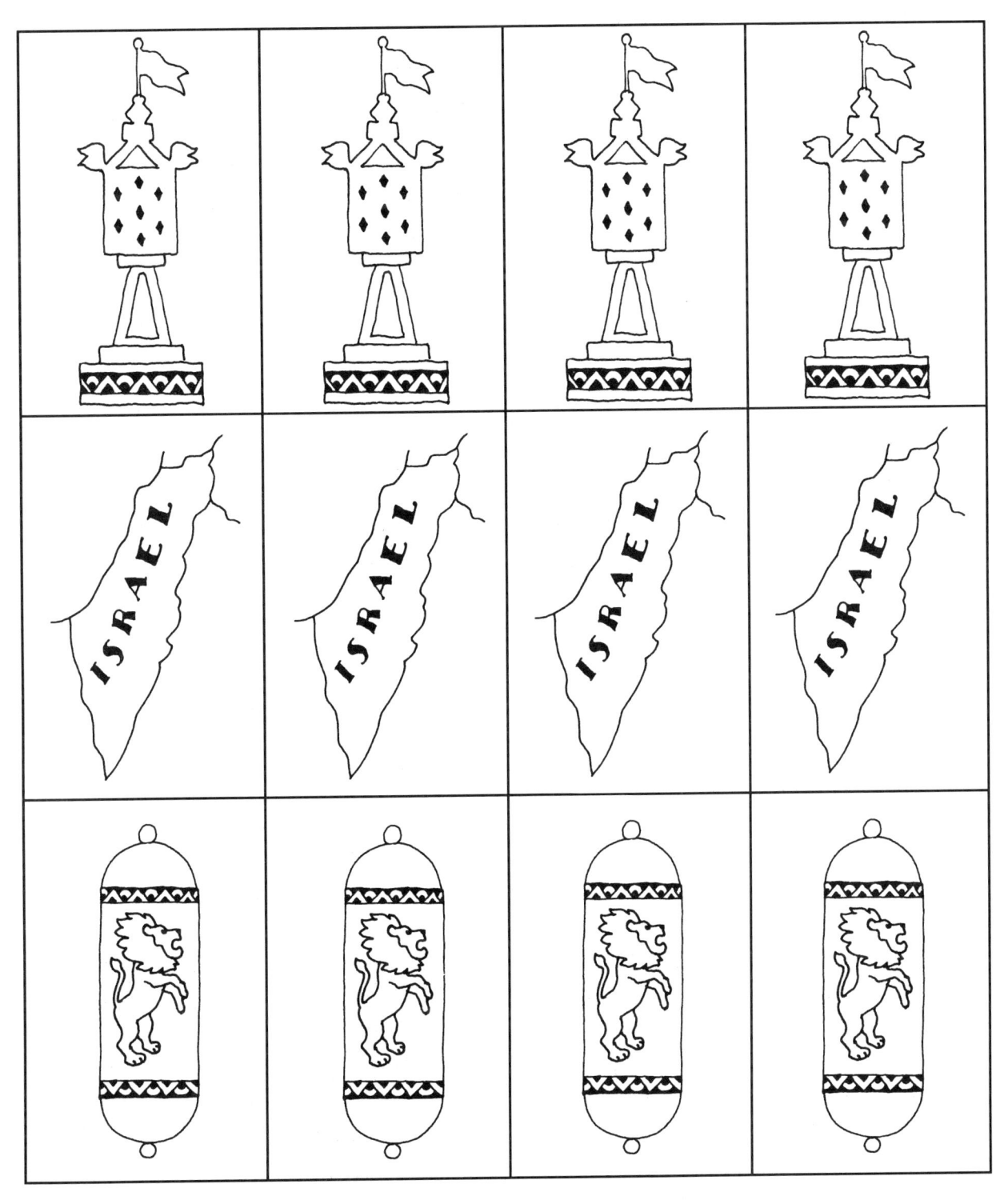

Welcoming the Sabbath
© The Learning Works, Inc.

Family Tikkun Olam Project

Tikkun olam is a Hebrew phrase that means "to mend the world." One Jewish scholar describes tikkun olam as "living your life in a way that makes others aware of G-d's presence in the world." Another calls it "to join with G-d in completing the work of creation." People participate in tikkun olam:

- by working for peace.
- by helping others in selfless ways.
- by making their way in the world as if they were personally responsible for making it a better place.

You perform an act of tikkun olam when you:

- give up your spare time to visit people who are too sick to leave their homes.
- clean up trash in a park.
- make a point of correcting a wrong that you or someone else has done.

You and your family can create a *tikkun olam* project.

1. Sit down together one Shabbat (or anytime). Talk about the problems you see in the community and the world. Talk about the small steps you might take to solve them. Here are some ideas for family *tikkun olam* projects:
   - Volunteer to serve food at a homeless shelter.
   - Organize a neighborhood garage sale for charity.
   - Plant a tree for every member of your family.
   - Collect and send food, clothes, and toys to children in countries troubled by war.

   What other ideas can you think of?

2. Decide on a *tikkun olam* project to do as a family. Talk about how you will organize your project. Let each family member have a job to do.

3. Make a promise to yourselves to follow through with the project by a certain date.

4. Take some time every Shabbat before that date to talk about your progress and discuss the next steps.

Jewish Community Worldwide

Share your family's Shabbat experiences with children in other communities. Find out how Jews around the world observe Shabbat. Here are two ways you can do this:

1. Find out from a synagogue, Jewish community center, or Jewish federation in your community how to locate pen pals in Israel and other places around the world. Trade stories about your family life and Shabbat experiences. Keep a notebook of all the different ways that people celebrate Shabbat.

2. Use the Internet to exchange news and greetings with Jewish families and communities around the world.

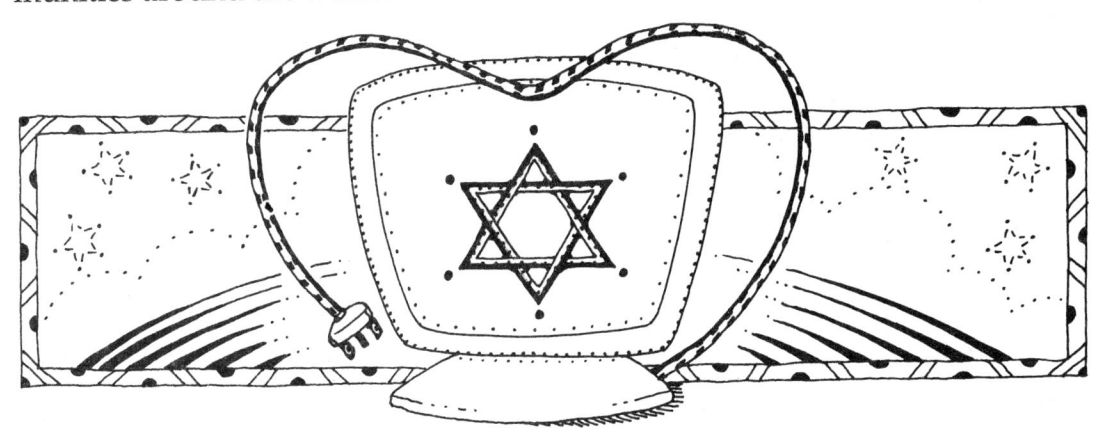

- Explore the Shamash home page with a parent:
    http://www.shamash.org

    This is a great starting point for finding Jewish resources on the Internet. Among them is a World Jewish Congress site, with links to Jewish communities in 120 countries. Most of the resources and information you'll find are for adults, but there are children-to-children exchanges, as well.

- Here are two more sites you can explore by yourself:

    Jewish Family Life Home Page
    http://www.jewishfamily.com

    Shabbat Shalom Home Page
    http://www.geocities.com/heartland/plains/7613

- Create your own family Web site—it's easier than you might think. You can post pictures, greetings to friends, and weekly news about how your family spent Shabbat.

Welcoming the Sabbath
© The Learning Works, Inc.

Family Shabbat Journal

Your whole family will enjoy participating in this project—an ongoing journal of your Shabbat experiences. It's a wonderful way to remember highlights of Shabbat over the years and your feelings about the holy day. You'll also be building a family heirloom that you will treasure for years to come.

1. Buy a notebook at a stationery store. A pad of paper will do, but just as you dress in your best clothes for Shabbat, you may want a special book for recording your Shabbat memories.

2. At the end of each Shabbat, any family member who wishes to may write an account of the day. Children who are too young to write can dictate their words to another family member. (The "scribe" should be sure to take down their words exactly, without changes.) Your entry may include anything about the day's experience, but here are a few suggestions:

   - Where did you have your Shabbat dinner? Were you at home, or were you guests in someone else's house? Who else was there? What did you eat? What happened that was special?

   - Did you or your family do anything during the day to remind you that it was Shabbat, and not an ordinary day?

   - Did anyone in your family observe any milestones during the week—anything from a bat mitzvah to a lost tooth?

   - Did anything happen to make you feel especially thankful to G-d?

3. Not everyone needs to write in your family Shabbat journal every week. However, suggest to your family each week that at least one person write in the journal.

4. When you've filled one notebook, get another one and continue your journal. Go back and leaf through old volumes from time to time. It can be as rewarding as looking at old home videos—and it's a lot less complicated!

Welcoming the Sabbath
© The Learning Works, Inc.

Arts and Crafts

Make a Challah Cover

Here is a festive challah cover you can make yourself.
(See pages 60–61 for a delicious challah recipe.)

What You Need

- white cotton or silk fabric, about 18 x 12" (to cover one loaf) or about 18 x 20" (to cover two)
- Hebrew alphabet patterns (page 57)
- pencil
- fabric paints and small paint brushes

optional:
- scraps of material of various colors
- needle and thread
- scissors

What You Do

1. Decide on a phrase to write on your challah cover, such as:

    Shabbat shalom   שבת שלום

    or

    hamotzi lechem min ha-aretz   המוציא לחם מן הארץ

    Carefully write the letters in pencil on the fabric. If you use Hebrew, outline the letters using the Hebrew alphabet patterns on page 57.

2. Use fabric paints to color in the letters.

3. Use the paints to further decorate the fabric as you wish. You might want to draw Stars of David, candlesticks, or other symbols of Shabbat.

You can also use fabric to decorate your cover. Using the alphabet patterns as a guide, outline the letters in pencil on scraps of fabric. Then cut the scraps of fabric to form the Hebrew letters that you want. Sew them in place on your challah cover. Use other scraps of material for more decoration.

Welcoming the Sabbath
© The Learning Works, Inc.

Hebrew Name Place Cards

Jewish children are given Hebrew names at birth. Sephardim traditionally name their children after living relatives, Ashkenazim after relatives who have died. For children with Biblical names such as David or Leah, the Hebrew name is often the same as the English name.

Here's how to use the Hebrew letter patterns on page 57 to make place cards for your family's Shabbat table.

What You Need

- blank cards, 5 x 7" or larger
- Hebrew alphabet patterns
- pencil
- wax crayons
- black paint or ink
- watercolor paints or markers
- small paint brushes
- stickers

What You Do

1. Find out the Hebrew name of every member of your family. Let anyone who doesn't have a Hebrew name choose one. Consult a Jewish name book, or choose a Hebrew name with a meaning similar to that of your English name.

2. For each place card, fold a blank card in half so that it will stand up. Use the alphabet patterns to trace the Hebrew name in pencil.

3. Use the crayons to color in the letters. Use several colors for each letter.

4. Cover the letters with the black paint or ink. Let dry.

5. Use the edge of the scissors to scratch patterns or shapes in the letters.

6. Use paints, markers, and stickers to decorate the area around the name.

Welcoming the Sabbath
© The Learning Works, Inc.

Twelve Tribes Cups

The symbols of the Twelve Tribes of Israel come from Jacob's blessing of his sons in Genesis 49. Serve your family and Shabbat guests wine or juice in cups decorated with these ancient symbols.

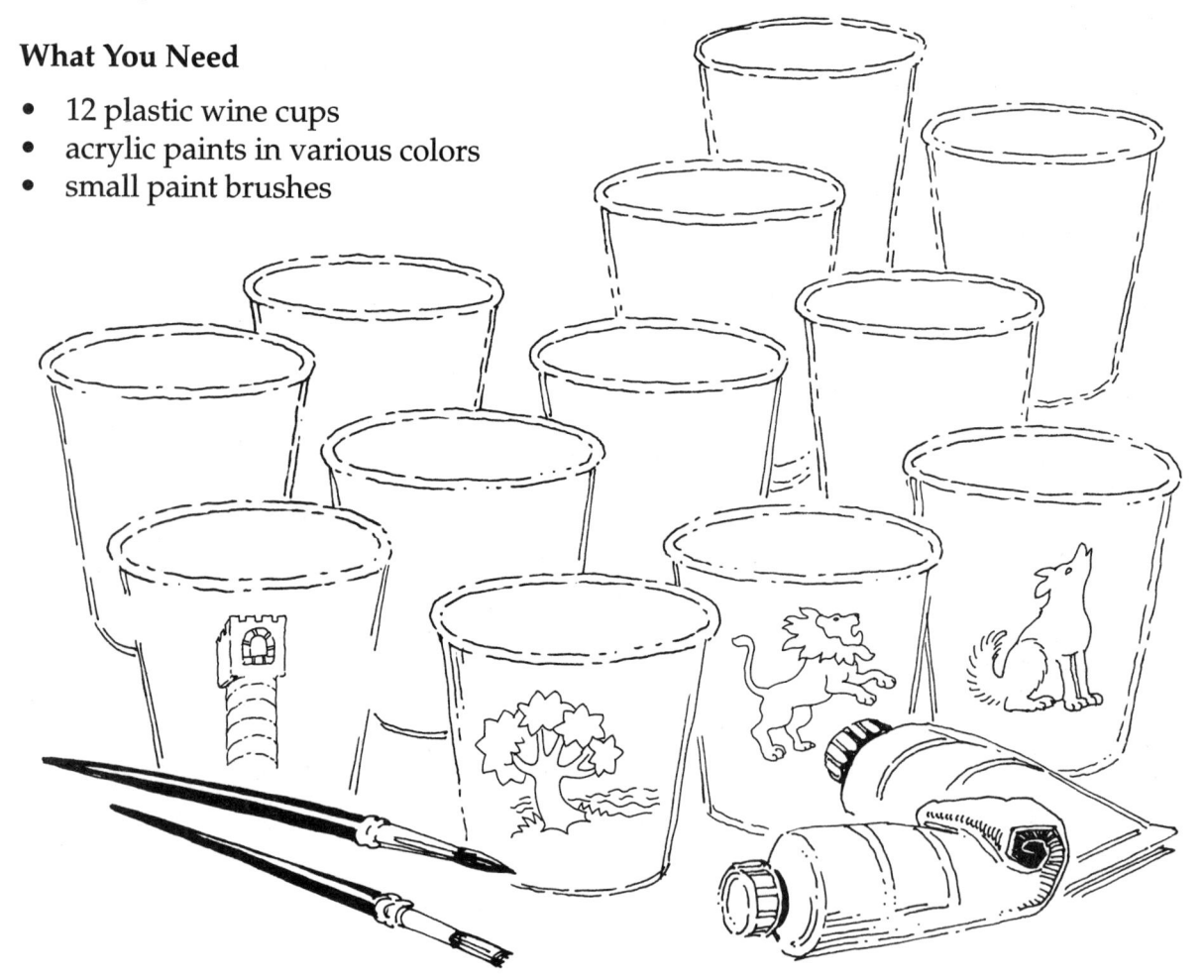

What You Need

- 12 plastic wine cups
- acrylic paints in various colors
- small paint brushes

What You Do

1. Use the illustrations on page 49 to guide you in drawing and painting the symbols of the 12 tribes: Reuven: a tree standing by water, Shimon: tower, Levi: breastplate of judgment in 12 sections, Judah: lion, Issakhar: sunburst with stars, Zevulun: ship, Dan: scales of justice, Naftali: deer, Gad: tents, Asher: apple tree, Joseph: sheaf of wheat, Benjamin: wolf.

2. If you wish, write the names of the tribes on your cups in Hebrew or English.

Welcoming the Sabbath
© The Learning Works, Inc.

Symbols of the Twelve Tribes of Israel

Reuven ראובן	Shimon שמעון	Levi לוי
Judah יהודה	Issakhar יששכר	Zevulun זבולון
Dan דן	Naftali נפתלי	Gad גד
Asher אשר	Joseph יוסף	Benjamin בנימן

Welcoming the Sabbath
© The Learning Works, Inc.

Make a Shabbat Mural

Here is an art project for the whole family: a mural-sized wall hanging with a Shabbat theme. You'll create pictures and group them together in one large "frame of reference." Hang it in your home as a reminder of your family life and your link with other Jews.

What You Need

- cardboard or poster board, 3 x 4' or larger, or a flat white bedsheet.
- drawing paper, paints, small brushes markers, fabric scraps and other art supplies (see below)
- family photographs
- white glue
- cellophane tape

What You Do

1. Let all family members contribute to this project. Everyone can help in the planning, with the following guidelines in mind:

    - Use Jewish subjects for the art—Shabbat and holidays, scenes from the Bible and from Jewish history, etc.
    - Use a variety of "flat" artistic media (no sculpture)—paint, colored pencils, markers, or chalk and fabric or colored paper to create collages.

2. Let participants create their artwork. You can also use artwork you've done previously, such as for a religious school or camp project. Finally, assemble a few family photos that would go well with the theme of the mural.

3. Use white glue and cellophane tape to affix the art to the background—the poster board, cardboard, or sheet.

4. Hang the mural on the wall. Add to it or change it as often as you wish.

Jewish Jigsaw Puzzle

Here's how to create your own Jewish jigsaw puzzle, suitable for you or your family to solve on a rainy Shabbat afternoon—or anytime you'd like to challenge your mind.

What You Need

- drawing paper
- poster board or cardboard
- watercolor or acrylic paints, or markers
- small paint brushes
- scissors
- white glue

What You Do

1. Make sure your drawing paper is the same size as the poster board or cardboard you'll use for the backing. If it isn't, cut it to fit.

2. Use paints or markers to create a colorful picture on drawing paper. Make it a scene from the Bible or from Jewish life. Let the paint dry.

3. Glue your painting to the cardboard or poster board. Use a thin layer of glue that covers the whole area. Let the glue dry.

4. Turn your picture face down. Cut it into as many pieces as you want.

5. Give your puzzle to a family member or friend to solve.

You may wish to have an adult cut your puzzle into pieces with a craft knife. (Don't try it yourself!) You can also paint your picture on a precut, blank jigsaw puzzle from an art-supply store or hobby shop.

Welcoming the Sabbath
© The Learning Works, Inc.

Scenes From the Parashiot

Every Shabbat morning, a portion of the Torah, or *parasha*, is read in the synagogue. The *parashiot* follow a yearly cycle that begins and ends on Simchat Torah. Each parasha contains a few chapters of Torah. The names of the parashiot are taken from the first word, or words, of the section. Every Shabbat is named for the parasha that is read on that day.

Here is a project that will help you learn about the Torah as you create art illustrating the parashiot.

What You Need

- Jewish Bible in English
- art paper, 8 1/2 x 11"
- binder or folder
- watercolor or acrylic paints, markers, colored pencils
- small paint brushes
- fabric
- white glue
- other art supplies as desired
- Hebrew alphabet patterns (page 57)

Welcoming the Sabbath
© The Learning Works, Inc.

Scenes From the Parashiot

What You Do

1. Read the parasha for the week, or choose any parasha from your Bible. (In an English translation, each parasha is headed by its name in Hebrew. A Jewish calendar will tell you which parasha is read on each Shabbat.)

2. Choose a scene from the parasha to illustrate. Draw more than one scene if you wish. Some parashiot contain familiar stories with lots of scenes to illustrate. Others are made up mostly of laws, but even these may suggest illustrations. For example, for the parasha *Sh'mini*, which tells which animals are kosher and which are not, you might draw a pig inside the familiar "no" symbol.

3. Use paints, markers, fabric, or other art supplies to create your illustration. If you wish, use the Hebrew alphabet patterns to write the name of the parasha on your illustration.

4. After you finish an illustration, put it in the binder or folder. Keep adding to your collection until you have illustrated every parasha in the Torah.

Stained-Glass Windows

If you've been to Israel, you may have seen the stained-glass windows in the Hadassah Hospital in Jerusalem. These "paintings in light" of scenes from the Bible were created by the artist Marc Chagall. Here is a way you can make your own stained-glass illustrations without glass—and without staining, either. Adorn your home with your favorite scenes from the Bible or from Jewish life.

What You Need

- construction paper
- waxed paper
- drawing paper
- colored acetate sheets
- pencil
- scissors
- white glue
- cellophane tape

What You Do

1. Cut two rectangles of equal size from construction paper. Cut a large space for the picture from both sheets, leaving the outside edges as a frame.

2. Carefully glue a piece of waxed paper to each frame, creating a large pane.

3. Draw your scene in pencil on the drawing paper.

4. Using your drawing as a guide, carefully trace and cut pieces of colored acetate to make your "stained-glass" shapes.

5. Place one waxed-paper pane over your drawing. Assemble the acetate pieces on the pane, using the drawing as a guide. Glue them in place with a thin line of white glue around the edges.

6. Glue the other frame over the one that holds the illustration. Let the frame dry.

7. Tape your creation to a sunny window.

Welcoming the Sabbath
© The Learning Works, Inc.

A Thousand Words Are Worth a Picture

"You shall not make for yourself a graven image, or any kind of likeness." Many traditional Jews have interpreted the Second Commandment as banning all forms of representational art—pictures, that is. Ah, but the written word—well, that was another matter. The word was holy. And if holy words happened to look like a landscape or Moses receiving the Torah, what was wrong with that? And so Jews developed *microtopography*—pictures made of words. They decorated books with pictures made up of tiny Hebrew letters. Often the pictures showed what the words described. One Israeli artist has created microtopographic pictures that use the text of a whole book of the Bible! You can start with something simpler—a torah scroll, perhaps, or a loaf of challah on a platter.

What You Need

- drawing paper
- pencil
- fine-point markers or colored pencils

What You Do

1. Outline your drawing lightly in pencil. You may want to use a color code to remember the colors of different sections of your drawing.

2. Using markers or colored pencils, outline and fill in each section of your drawing with tiny words. Use either Hebrew or English letters.

3. Make the words match the picture. For example, if your picture shows your mother lighting the Shabbat candles, use the words "l'hadlik ner shel Shabbat" over and over.

Mezuzah Growth Chart

Many families mark the growth of their children in pencil on a wall. Here's a growth chart you can make for yourself, for a younger brother or sister, or as a present for a family with a new baby.

What You Need
- piece of felt or burlap 5'6" or longer and 10" wide
- 12" length of $1/2$" dowel
- trimmings (such as ribbon or rickrack)
- permanent markers in various colors
- Hebrew alphabet patterns (page 57)
- 36" cloth tape measure
- small pieces of fabric
- white glue
- scissors

What You Do

1. Wrap one end of the long piece of fabric around the dowel. Glue it in place to form a loop.

2. Use markers to draw lines around the edge of the fabric to form a mezuzah shape.

3. Carefully measure two feet from the bottom of the fabric (opposite the dowel). Glue the tape measure along the center of the fabric starting at that point. Cut fabric scraps or use markers to mark "2 feet" at the bottom of the tape measure. Mark "3 feet," "4 feet," and "5 feet" at the 12", 24", and 36" marks.

4. Use markers and the Hebrew alphabet patterns to write your Hebrew name or another child's name near the top.

5. Use the markers and fabric to decorate the chart with Stars of David, torah scrolls, and other Jewish symbols. Use the trimmings for further decoration.

6. Using push pins or tacks to support the dowel, hang the growth chart on the wall. The bottom should be just touching the floor.

7. Use markers to record both growth and Jewish milestones such as bar- or bat mitzvahs and the first time the four questions are recited at Passover.

Welcoming the Sabbath
© The Learning Works, Inc.

Hebrew Alphabet Patterns

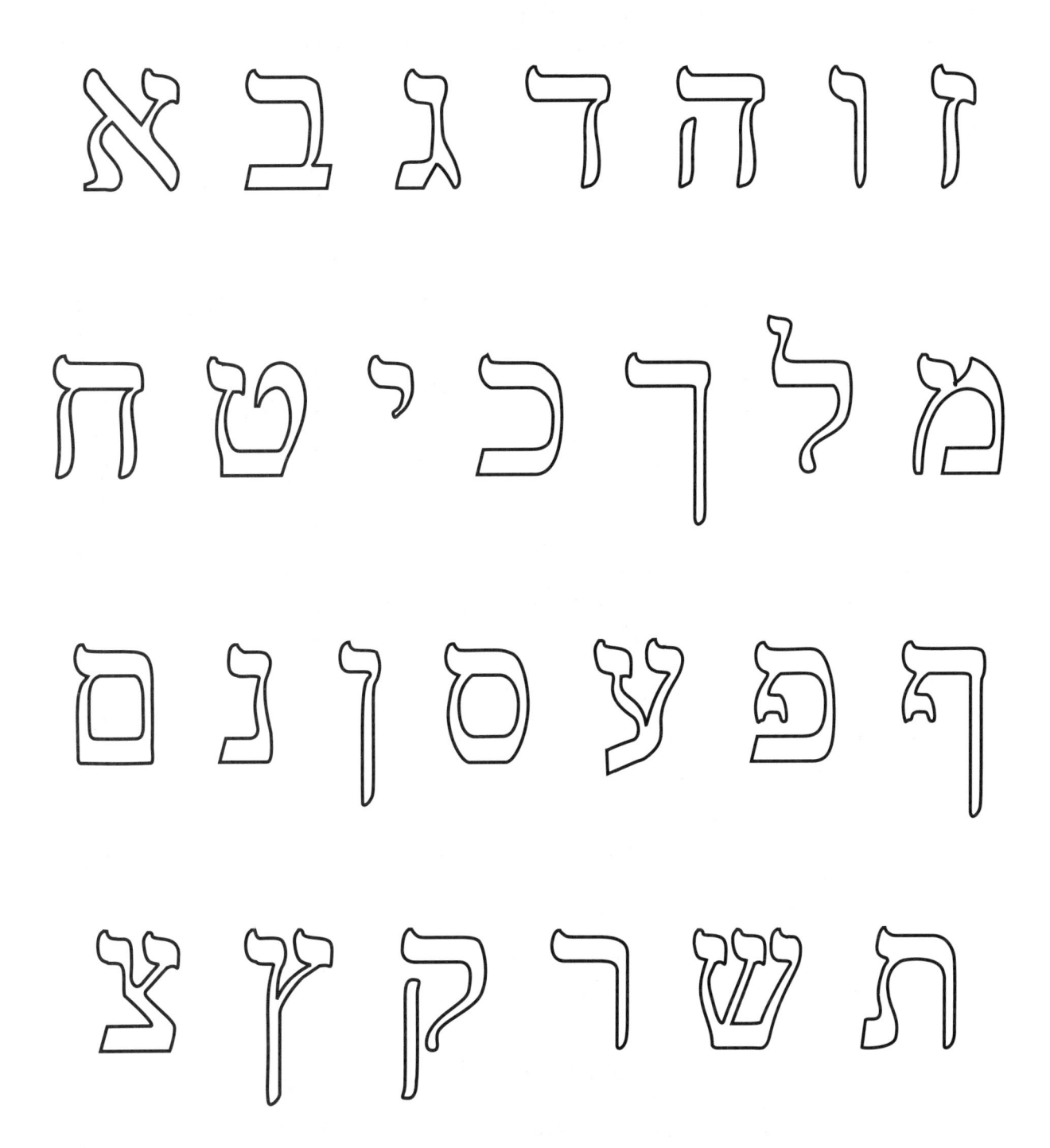

זוהדגבא

מלךכיטחח

ףפעסונםמ

תשרקץצ

Make Havdalah Candles

In some families, secrets for making havdalah candles are passed along from generation to generation. But you don't need any secret recipes. Here is a quick and easy way to do it.

What You Need
- wicking
- beeswax sheets
- scissors
- warm water

What You Do

1. Cut the beeswax lengthwise into narrow strips. You'll need three strips for each candle.

2. Cut three lengths of wick about $1/4$–$1/2$" longer than the wax strips.

3. Dip a strip of beeswax into warm water for a few seconds. Take it out. Lay a wick along one edge so that one end of the wick is even with the end of the wax strip. This is the bottom. The other end of the wick should stick out a little at the top.

4. Roll up the wax into a tube, trapping the wick inside.

5. Repeat steps three and four tor the other two strips.

6. Braid the three strips together, starting from the bottom.

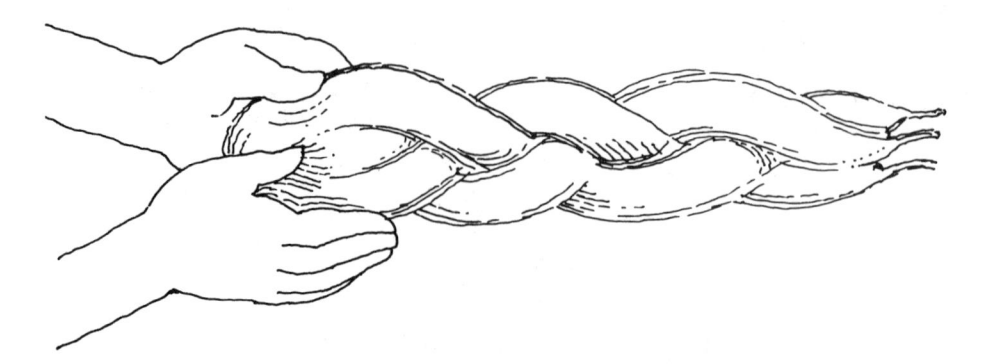

7. Squeeze the bottom of the braid together. (You don't need to set a havdalah candle in a candlestick, so it doesn't matter how thick it is.) Gently pinch the braid together all the way up so that the candle will burn better.

Welcoming the Sabbath
© The Learning Works, Inc.

Recipes

Challah for Shabbat

The Hebrew word *challah* means "set aside." Originally, the word referred to the dough set aside for the priests in the Temple in Jerusalem. It has long been the name for the traditional egg bread eaten on Shabbat.

Challah is made with eggs instead of milk so that observant Jews may eat it with meat. In many Jewish communities of the past, meat was a luxury. This is why challah is associated with Shabbat and other festive occasions, while humbler breads baked with milk are eaten during the week.

What You Need *(for one large loaf)*

- 1 package dry yeast
- pinch of sugar
- 3 large eggs
- 1/2 teaspoon salt
- 1 tablespoon vegetable oil
- 1/3 cup honey
- 4 cups unbleached white flour

What You Do

1. Dissolve yeast in 1 cup warm water. Add the sugar and stir. Set aside until the liquid foams.

2. Separate one of the eggs. Set the yolk aside. Beat the white together with the other two eggs. Add the salt, oil, and honey. Keep beating the mixture.

Challah for Shabbat

3. Put the flour in a large bowl. Add the yeast mixture slowly and mix thoroughly with a hand mixer. Then stir in the egg mixture.

4. Knead the dough. If it is sticky, sprinkle on a little flour. Cover the bowl with a dish towel. Let it stand in a warm spot for about 2 hours. Then punch it down to about half its size.

5. Shape the dough into six ropes. Three of them should be about 12 inches long, the other three a little shorter. Braid the 12-inch pieces and press them together at the ends. Then braid the shorter pieces and place them on top of the longer ones. Press the ends together.

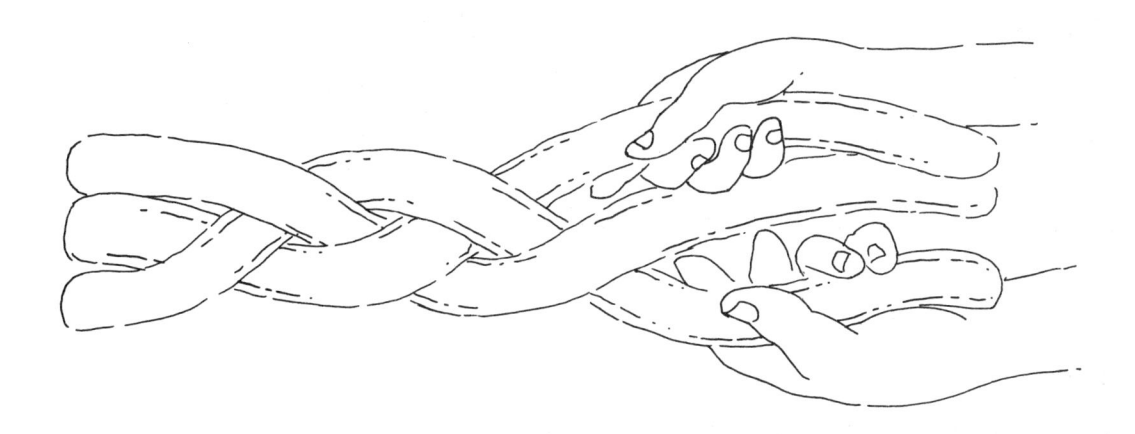

6. Mix the egg yolk you saved in step 2 with 1 teaspoon of cold water. Brush the egg yolk on the braided dough as a glaze. Leave it uncovered for 1 hour.

7. Preheat the oven to 375°. Bake for 20–25 minutes or until bread is golden brown.

A Little Chicken Soup

Your parents or grandparents may joke about chicken soup. That's because *their* grandparents probably offered it to them as the best medicine for everything from colds to skinned knees. Here are two recipes.

Note: This activity requires adult supervision.

Ashkenazic Chicken Soup

What You Need

- 1 whole chicken, cut up
- 2 carrots
- 1 medium onion
- 3 stalks of celery
- salt and pepper to taste
- 1 cup thin egg noodles (optional)

What You Do

1. Cut vegetables into large pieces. In a large pot, cover the chicken pieces with 8–10 cups water. Add the vegetables, salt, and pepper. Bring everything to a boil. Then lower the heat and simmer for two hours.

2. Remove all but one of the chicken pieces to serve separately. Cut the remaining piece into bite-sized bits and return them to the soup. Taste; add more salt and pepper if necessary. Add the noodles if you wish and simmer for another 5 minutes, or until the noodles are tender.

A Little Chicken Soup

Sephardic Chicken Soup

What You Need

- 1 whole chicken, cut up
- 1/2 cup white beans
- 2 zucchini
- 2 carrots
- 2 medium-sized potatoes
- 2 onions
- 2 tomatoes
- salt and pepper to taste
- 1 cup thin egg noodles (optional)

What You Do

1. Soak beans overnight, or about 8–10 hours.

2. Cut vegetables into large pieces. Put the vegetables and beans into a large pot. Add the chicken pieces, salt, and pepper. Cover with about 10 cups of water. Bring everything to a boil. Then lower the heat and simmer for 2–3 hours.

3. Remove the tomatoes. Taste; add more salt and pepper if necessary. Add the noodles if you wish and simmer for another 5 minutes, or until the noodles are tender.

Liverless Chopped Liver

Mmmm! Chicken liver chopped with onions and hard-boiled eggs was a favorite of Jews in Europe and America for generations. What made it especially yummy was gobs of golden *schmalz* (chicken fat), just loaded with calories and cholesterol! Jews today still enjoy traditional chopped liver, but in our diet-conscious age we may prefer a healthier choice. Try this substitute on your great-aunt Sylvia from Brooklyn. She'll swear it tastes like the real thing!

Note: This activity requires adult supervision.

What You Need

- 1/2 cup lentils
- 1/4 cup walnuts
- 1 medium onion
- 1/4 cup cooking oil
- 1 tablespoon chicken-soup granules
- 1 teaspoon beef granules
- white of 1 hard-boiled egg

What You Do

1. Cook the lentils in 2 cups of water for about 20 minutes or until soft. Drain well in a strainer.

2. Slice the onion. Heat the oil in a frying pan until it's very hot. Fry the onion quickly, stirring constantly with a spatula or wooden spoon until the onion begins to turn golden brown.

3. Place the lentils, onion, walnuts, chicken-soup granules, beef granules, and egg white in a food processor. Process until smooth.

4. Chill in the refrigerator. Spread on challah or your favorite crackers.

Tabbuleh

Here's a colorful Israeli favorite for your Shabbat afternoon meal. It's also an easy salad to make for the festive meal on Shabbat eve.

Note: This activity requires adult supervision.

What You Need

- 1 cup bulgur wheat
- 1 1/2 cups cold water
- 1 clove garlic, minced
- 1/4 teaspoon grated onion
- 1 1/2 tablespoons lemon juice
- 2 1/2–3 tablespoons olive oil
- 1 large tomato, finely diced
- handful of parsley, chopped (you may substitute Italian parsley, or combine both)
- pita bread

What You Do

1. Pour the water over the bulgur wheat in a bowl.

2. Add the garlic and onion. (Pass a raw onion across a grater once or twice over the bowl.) Set aside for about half an hour.

3. Add the other vegetables, lemon juice, and olive oil. Stir well.

4. Scoop up with pita bread to eat.

Roast Chicken and Vegetables

Here's a delicious and easy main course for your Shabbat dinner. Roast brisket of beef or baked fish are also traditional favorites, and vegetarian dishes turn up on Shabbat tables too, but chicken is still number one.

Note: This activity requires adult supervision.

What You Need

- 4 carrots
- 4 potatoes
- 1 large onion, peeled
- 1 turnip or 2 parsnips
- 3 tablespoons olive oil
- 1/2 tablespoon dried rosemary
- 1 whole roasting chicken, 3 1/2–4 pounds
- 1 lemon, cut in half
- canola or other vegetable oil
- salt and pepper

What You Do

1. Preheat the oven to 375°. Cut the potatoes and the onion in quarters. Cut the other vegetables into bite-sized pieces.

2. Put the vegetables, olive oil, and rosemary in a casserole or clay pot with the olive oil. Sprinkle with salt and pepper. Stir well to coat all the vegetable pieces with the oil. Cover and place in oven.

3. Rub the chicken with a damp cloth. Brush or spoon on a small amount of vegetable oil. Rub the inside of the chicken with vegetable oil and half of the lemon.

Roast Chicken and Vegetables

4. Place the chicken on one side on a rack in a shallow roasting pan. Roast for 25 minutes.

5. Baste the chicken with pan juices. Using a long fork or tongs, turn the chicken on its other side and roast for another 25 minutes.

6. Baste the chicken again. Carefully uncover the vegetables with an oven mitt and baste them with the pan juices. Replace the cover. Turn the chicken on its back and baste again. Let it roast for another 15 minutes.

7. Baste the chicken again and sprinkle with salt. Continue roasting for another 15 minutes.

8. Take the vegetables out of the oven and set aside, covered. Take the chicken out and let it sit on a hot platter for about 10 minutes.

9. Have an adult carve the chicken. Serve and eat!

Bubbe's Mandelbroit

And now for dessert! *Mandelbroit* means "almond nut bread" in Yiddish, but it's really a kind of cookie. This recipe makes enough for the whole family to pack in their lunch boxes for the first few days of the week. Be sure that you have three 4 1/2 x 9" baking pans—the size used for meat loaf.

Note: This activity requires adult supervision.

What You Need

- 4 eggs
- 1 1/2 cups sugar
- 1 teaspoon vanilla extract
- 1/2 teaspoon almond extract
- cinnamon (pinch)
- 1/2 cup canola oil or other vegetable oil
- 3 cups unbleached white flour
- 1 tablespoon baking powder
- 1/4 teaspoon salt
- 1/4 teaspoon grated lemon rind
- 1 cup almonds
- oil or vegetable shortening

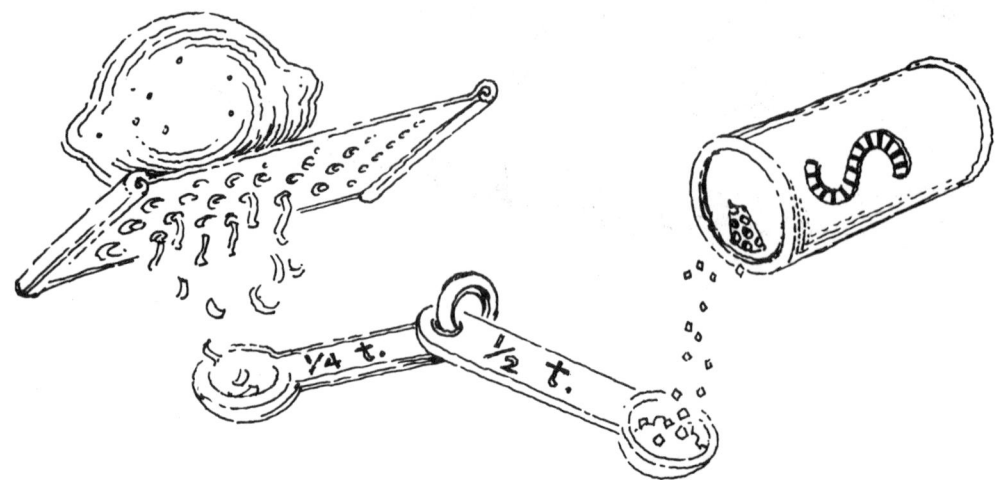

Bubbe's Mandelbroit

What You Do

1. Preheat the oven to 350°.

2. Beat together the eggs, sugar, vanilla and almond extracts, and cinnamon. Add the 1/2 cup oil and beat some more.

3. In a separate bowl, sift the flour, baking powder, and salt together. Add the grated lemon rind.

4. Fold the flour mixture into the egg mixture. Use a hand mixer to blend them together thoroughly.

5. Chop the almonds coarsely in a blender or food processor. Mix them thoroughly with the dough.

6. Wipe the cooking pans with oil or shortening. Pour the dough into the pans about 1 inch deep. Bake 45 minutes.

7. Remove from the oven and cut into slices.

Favorite Fruit Salads

This is probably the easiest recipe you'll ever make. It's so easy, in fact, that we've included two. The first contains fruits that are mentioned in the Bible or are traditionally grown in Israel. The second is more of an all-American fruit salad.

Israeli Fruit Salad

What You Need

- 1 cantaloupe
- 3 large apples
- 3 oranges, peeled
- 1/2 cup seedless grapes
- 1/2 cup raisins
- 1 fig

What You Do

1. Cut the melon into bite-sized pieces, or use a melon baller. Cut the apples, oranges, and fig into bite-sized pieces.
2. Mix the pieces together in a bowl with the grapes and raisins.
3. Serve with a bowl of low-fat yogurt.

Everything-but-the-Kitchen-Sink Fruit Salad

What You Need

- 2 apples
- 1 pear
- 1 orange, peeled
- 1 kiwi, peeled
- 1 ripe peach
- 1 generous slice of watermelon
- 2 bananas
- 5 strawberries
- 1/2 cup seedless grapes
- 1/2 cup raisins
- 1/2 cup blueberries
- 1/2 cup chopped walnuts
- any other fruit you choose

What You Do

1. Cut the apples, pear, orange, kiwi and peach into bite-sized pieces.
2. Cut the watermelon into bite-sized pieces, carefully removing the seeds. Put into a bowl with the apple mixture.
3. Thinly slice the bananas and strawberries. Add them to the bowl.
4. Add the grapes, raisins, walnuts, and blueberries, and mix well.
5. Serve with a bowl of low-fat yogurt.

Hummos

Here is an Israeli favorite to enjoy with challah on Shabbat afternoon, or with pita anytime. *Hummos* is actually the Hebrew (and the Arabic) word for chick peas. (They're called garbanzo beans or ceci beans in some places.) Here's how to turn a simple bean into a delicious dip or spread.

Note: This activity requires adult supervision.

What You Need

- 1 cup dried (or 15 ounces canned) chick peas
- 1/4 teaspoon salt
- 6 tablespoons tehina (sesame butter)
- 2 cloves garlic, minced
- 5 tablespoons lemon juice
- 3 tablespoons olive oil
- 1/4 teaspoon paprika

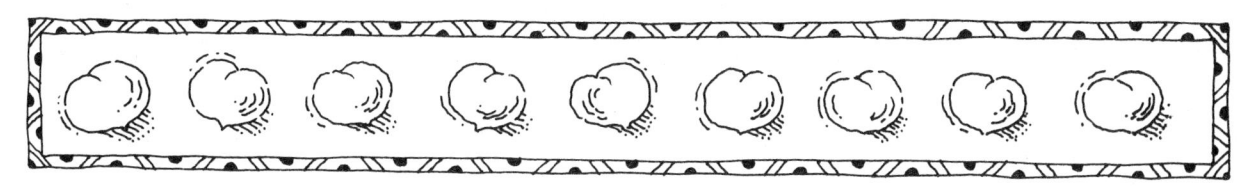

What You Do

Note: If you use canned chick peas, skip steps 1–3.

1. Let dried chick peas soak overnight in water. Pour off the liquid.

2. Put the beans in a pot, cover them with fresh water, and bring to a boil.

3. Lower the heat so that the water is just bubbling. Add 1/4 teaspoon of the salt. Cook 1 1/2 to 2 hours, or until the beans are soft.

4. Drain off the cooking liquid, or the liquid in the can, and set it aside for later.

5. Put the beans in a food processor with the tehina, garlic, lemon juice, olive oil, 1/4 teaspoon salt, and the paprika. (If you like hot and spicy foods, substitute a little cayenne pepper for some of the paprika.) You may want to turn the jar of tehina upside down for a few minutes before you spoon it out so that the oil and sesame paste are well mixed.

6. Process in a food processor or blender until smooth. You may want to add more olive oil or some of the liquid you drained from the chick peas to make it creamier.

7. Taste. You may decide that you want to add a little more of something. Chill in the refrigerator before serving.

Baklava

Baklava is a delicious dessert that's a favorite in Israel and all across the Middle East. You might be able to make it yourself, but you'll probably want an adult to help you.

What You Need

- 1-pound box filo (phyllo) dough
- 1 pound mixed almonds and walnuts, ground
- 1 cup granulated (white) sugar
- 2 teaspoons ground cinnamon
- 1/2 teaspoon ground cardamom seed
- 1/8 teaspoon ground cloves
- 1/2 pound unsalted butter or margarine
- vegetable shortening
- 1/2 cup brown sugar
- 1/2 cup honey
- 1/3 cup lemon juice
- 1 cup water

What You Do

1. Preheat oven to 350°.
2. Combine the ground nuts in a bowl with the white sugar and cinnamon. Stir.
3. Melt the butter or margarine over a low heat. Do not burn.
4. Lightly grease a 12 x 17" cake pan with the vegetable shortening. Fold 4 sheets of filo dough in half to form 8 layers. Put them in the bottom of the pan. Brush melted butter between each layer.
5. Spread a layer of the nut mixture evenly along the top sheet. Add 6 more layers of filo, brushing melted butter between each layer. Repeat this step until you reach the top of the pan. Spread the rest of the melted butter evenly across the top.
6. Cut into squares. Bake 45 minutes.
7. While the pastry is baking, mix the brown sugar, honey, lemon juice, water, cardamom, and cloves in a pot. Boil for 15 minutes, stirring, until you have a thick syrup. Let cool.
8. Pour the syrup over the baked pastry. Let the baklava stand for about an hour before serving.

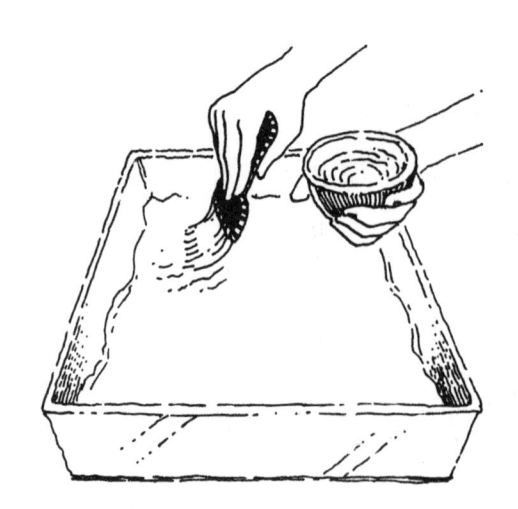

Welcoming the Sabbath
© The Learning Works, Inc.